QuickBooks® All-in-One Desk Reference For Dummies® 2nd Edition

W9-BEZ-384

Speedy Keyboard Shortcuts

Shortcut Key Combination	Result
Ctrl+A	Displays the Chart of Accounts window
Ctrl+C	Copies your selection to the clipboard
Ctrl+F	Displays the Find window
Ctrl+G	Goes to the other side of a transfer transaction
Ctrl+I	Displays the Create Invoice window
Ctrl+J	Displays the Customer:Job List window
Ctrl+M	Memorizes a transaction
Ctrl+N	Creates a new *<form>* where *form* is whatever is active at the time
Ctrl+P	Almost always prints the currently active register, list, or form
Ctrl+Q	Creates and displays a QuickReport on the selected transaction
Ctrl+R	Displays the Register window
Crtl+T	Displays the memorized transaction list
Ctrl+V	Pastes the contents of the clipboard
Ctrl+W	Displays the Write Checks window
Ctrl+X	Moves your selection to the clipboard
Ctrl+Z	Undoes your last action — usually
Ctrl+Ins	Inserts a line into a list of items or expenses
Ctrl+Del	Deletes the selected line from a list of items or expenses

How to Perform Common Tasks

To perform a common accounting or bookkeeping task, use these commands. When QuickBooks displays the commands window, you just fill in the boxes and press Enter.

To Do This	Choose This Command
Dealing with Customers	
Invoice a customer	Customers⇨Create Invoices
Record a cash sale	Customers⇨Enter Cash Receipts
Issue a credit memo	Customers⇨Create Credit Memo/Refunds
Record a customer payment	Customers⇨Receive Payments

Copyright © 2005 Wiley Publishing, Inc. All rights reserved.

Item 7662-3.

For more information about Wiley Publishing, call 1-800-762-2974.

For Dummies: Bestselling Book Series for Beginners

QuickBooks® All-in-One Desk Reference For Dummies, 2nd Edition

Cheat Sheet

How to Perform Common Tasks (continued)

To Do This	Choose This Command
Banking Activities	
Pay a bill with a check	Banking⇨Write Checks
Buy inventory with a check	Banking⇨Write Checks
Move money between bank accounts	Banking⇨Transfer Funds
Deposit money in a bank account	Banking⇨Make Deposit
See a bank account's transactions	Banking⇨Use Register
Reconcile a bank account	Banking⇨Reconcile
Working with Vendors	
Prepare a purchase order	Vendors⇨Create Purchase Orders
Record when items are received	Vendors⇨Receive Items or Vendors⇨Receive Items and Enter Bill
Record an accounts payable amount	Vendors⇨Enter Bills or Vendors⇨Enter Bills for Received Items
Managing Employees	
Preparing employee payroll	Employees⇨Pay Employees
Paying tax deposits	Employees⇨Pay Liabilities
Updating tax tables	Employees⇨Get Updates⇨Get Updates
Getting Financial Information	
Accounts	Lists⇨Chart of Accounts
Customers	Lists⇨Customer:Job List
Inventory	Lists⇨Item List
Vendors	Lists⇨Vendor List
Employees	Lists⇨Employee List
Managing Employees	
Profit and loss	Reports⇨Company & Financial⇨Profit & Loss Standard or one of the other profit & loss reports on Company & Financial submenu
Net worth	Reports⇨Company & Financial⇨Balance Sheet Standard or one of the other balance sheet reports on the Company & Financial submenu
Managing the QuickBooks System	
Setting up a new company	File⇨New Company
Resetting company information	Company⇨Company Information
Backing up data file	File⇨Back Up
Restoring a data file	File⇨Restore
Customizing QuickBooks	Edit⇨Preferences
Adjusting accounting data	Company⇨Make Journal Entry

For Dummies: Bestselling Book Series for Beginners

QuickBooks®

ALL-IN-ONE DESK REFERENCE

FOR

DUMMIES®

2ND EDITION